PRIMARY SOURCES OF REVOLUTIONARY
SCIENTIFIC DISCOVERIES AND THEORIES™

# WATSON AND CRICK
# AND DNA

CHRISTY MARX

rosen central
Primary Source™
The Rosen Publishing Group, Inc., New York

*For James Watson and in memory of Francis Crick, and all the great scientists who have explored and enlightened the human condition.*

Published in 2005 by The Rosen Publishing Group, Inc.
29 East 21st Street, New York, NY 10010

First Edition

**Library of Congress Cataloging-in-Publication Data**

Marx, Christy.
Watson and Crick and DNA / by Christy Marx.
    p. cm. — (Primary sources of revolutionary scientific discoveries and theories)
Includes bibliographical references and index.
ISBN 1-4042-0312-5 (library binding)
1. Crick, Francis, 1916–2004—Juvenile literature. 2. Watson, James D., 1928–—Juvenile literature. 3. DNA—Research—History—Juvenile literature. 4. Molecular biologists—Biography—Juvenile literature.
I. Title. II. Series.
QP624.M366 2004
572.8'6—dc22

                                                              2004011368

*Printed in Hong Kong*

**On the front cover:** A photograph of James Watson *(left)* and Francis Crick *(right)*.

**On the back cover:** Top to bottom: Nicolaus Copernicus, Charles Darwin, Edwin Hubble, Johannes Kepler, Gregor Mendel, Dmitry Mendeleyev, Isaac Newton, James Watson *(right)* and Francis Crick *(left)*.

# CONTENTS

# INTRODUCTION

For thousands of years, the human race has sought to understand how we grow and develop, what factors cause disease, and how our physical makeup affects our mental and emotional responses.

It was easy enough for people to observe that physical traits, such as eye color, hair color, skin color, and facial features, were passed on from parent to child, but no one understood how or why this happened.

## THE HUMAN MYSTERY

The mystery was finally solved during the second half of the twentieth century.

Scientists from many different scientific disciplines have contributed to the discovery and understanding of deoxyribonucleic acid, commonly known as DNA.

DNA is the genetic code hidden within cells that determines exactly how a living organism will develop, grow, and replicate (make a copy of itself).

Two men played a crucial role in unlocking this genetic code. James Dewey Watson and Francis Harry Compton Crick came from different parts of the world with very different attitudes. Watson was a bold young American who had already earned his Ph.D. in zoology (the study of animals), but he was something of a fish out of water when he arrived to work in the scientific circles of England. Crick, an English chemist, was twelve years older than

Long before the discovery of DNA, humankind knew about the phenomenon that allows for certain traits to be passed down from parents to children. In the mid-1800s, Gregor Mendel labeled these traits as genes. In the 1940s, DNA was identified as the substance that carries this genetic material. However, it wasn't until the work of James Watson and Francis Crick, who were able to crack the genetic code and discover the molecular structure of DNA, did we begin to fully understand DNA. This model, created by Dr. Van R. Potter, captures Watson and Crick's DNA model.

Watson but still hadn't earned his Ph.D. He was considered brilliant but loud and brash.

These two very different men found that they shared a personal ambition to be the first to solve the mystery of DNA. In the end, they arrived at the finish line together. Crick later noted in his book *What Mad Pursuit* that their success was "partly a matter of luck and partly good judgment, inspiration, and persistent application."

This is the story of how they did it.

# CHAPTER 1

**A**nne Elizabeth Crick had a few superstitious quirks. When her first son, Francis Harry, was born at home in Northampton, England, on June 8, 1916, Anne had the newborn baby carried to the top of the house so that later in life he would "rise to the top."

The Cricks were a comfortable middle-class family. Harry Crick, Francis's father, ran a boot and shoe factory with Francis's uncle. Young Francis was a fair-haired, blue-eyed child with an insatiable curiosity for science.

# TWO UNUSUAL MEN

### Blowing Things Up

When Francis was at an early age, his parents bought him the *Children's Encyclopedia*, a popular source of endless information. Francis was especially fascinated by anything having to do with science, but he worried that everything about science would already be known by the time he grew up. His mother assured him not to worry, that there would be plenty left for him to find out.

Around age ten, Francis began conducting experiments by putting chemicals into bottles and blowing them up using electricity. This led to a parental decree that he could blow up bottles only if they were immersed in water. His parents must have thought that would be safer!

Born in Northampton, England, in 1916, Francis Crick studied physics at University College in London. In 1937, he began research for his Ph.D., but this work was halted due to the onset of World War II (1939–1945). Following the war, he spent much of his time learning organic chemistry and crystallography, or the scientific study of crystals. It was during these years that Crick began working with the general theory of X-ray diffraction by a helix (the scattering of X-rays to discover how the atoms of a material are arranged). These studies would greatly aid him and his partner, James Watson, in their quest for the structure of DNA.

## Derailed by War

As a young man, Crick attended University College in London, where he earned a bachelor of science degree in physics. In 1939, World War II erupted throughout Europe. Crick went to work for the British navy designing magnetic and acoustic mines to sink enemy ships. During this time, Crick married his first wife, Doreen. A son was born to the couple during an air raid in 1940, when the German military devastated England with relentless bombings.

## The Gossip Test

After the war, Crick didn't want to keep designing weapons. He finally decided upon a course to follow by what he called the

Like many scientists of the time, Francis Crick lent his great mind to the effort of defeating the Axis powers during World War II. Even pacifists, like the brilliant physicist Albert Einstein *(above right)* pitched in during the war years. Here, Einstein speaks with Captain Geoffrey E. Sage and Lieutenant Commander Frederick L. Douthit of the U.S. Army in Princeton, New Jersey, in 1943. In 1939, Einstein formally abandoned his pacifist ways and personally wrote to President Franklin D. Roosevelt, pleading with Roosevelt to accelerate the United States' development of nuclear weapons. However, Einstein never supported dropping the atomic bombs on Japan in 1945.

Gossip Test. Crick paid attention to what he would gossip about with his friends. By "gossip," he meant whatever subject he talked about most often and with the most enthusiasm. He discovered that what he liked to talk about the most was the borderline between the living and the nonliving, a science we know today as molecular biology.

# Change of Direction

Crick first went to work at Strangeways Laboratory in Cambridge, England, in 1947. There, he investigated what effect magnetism might have on cytoplasm (the jellylike material inside a cell excluding its nucleus). It has since been determined that DNA is sensitive to magnetic fields because DNA itself is electrically charged. DNA has both a negative pole and a positive pole, the same as a magnet. That is why exposing an organism to a strong electromagnetic field can damage DNA.

By 1949, Crick was doing research at the Cavendish Laboratory in Cambridge, where he studied the structures of protein, the long-chained molecules that build and repair cells. During this time, he had to teach himself, from scratch, everything he could about biology, organic chemistry (the study of matter derived from natural sources), and X-ray diffraction technology (also known as X-ray crystallography). Each of these principles would become vital to the eventual understanding of the structure of DNA.

## MOLECULAR BIOLOGY

Biology is the study of living organisms. Molecular biology is specifically the study of the smallest unit of a chemical compound (a molecule) within a living organism. It is the boundary where chemical processes become the processes that allow life to exist. For example, when we digest food, it is converted into energy for our body. When we cut ourselves, chemical processes tell the cells how to repair themselves and heal the cut.

James Watson was born in Chicago in 1928 and was an only child. He received his bachelor's degree from the University of Chicago in 1947 and three years later earned his Ph.D. from Indiana University. During these years, his interest in genetics became a full-grown obsession. While performing research at the University of Copenhagen in Denmark, he first learned of the biomolecular research under way at the Cavendish Laboratory in Cambridge, England. It was there that Watson would meet Francis Crick.

During this time, Crick divorced Doreen and married his second wife, Odile, with whom he would have two daughters. One day, Odile came home and said that she'd met an American named Jim Watson and that he had no hair. What she meant was that he had an American crew cut, a style that was considered strange in Cambridge at the time.

## James Watson

In contrast to Crick's interest, Watson's fascination with genetics began at an early age. James Watson was born in Chicago, Illinois, on April 6, 1928, to James and Jean Watson. The young Jim Watson wasn't interested in being a kid. He wanted to grow up as quickly as possible to take part in adult activities. From the start, he was highly competitive.

By the age of twelve, Jim was appearing on a popular radio show called *Quiz Kids*, which posed difficult questions for kids to answer.

Jim graduated from high school and entered the University of Chicago at the age of fifteen. He was an avid bird-watcher and was fascinated by the phenomenon of bird migration, so he majored in zoology.

## Fascinated by Genetics

In 1947, Watson was invited to join a group of scientists who shared the same interest in studying bacteriophages ("phages" for short), which are a type of virus that preys on bacteria. These scientists called themselves the Phage Group.

Watson was heavily influenced by a book entitled *What Is Life?* by theoretical physicist Erwin Schrödinger. In it, Schrödinger puts forth the idea that to understand what life is, it is necessary to know

## X-RAYS AND X-RAY DIFFRACTION

X-rays can pass through almost anything except lead and other very dense materials. X-rays pass through soft tissue more easily than hard tissue, which is why they're used to take images of bones and teeth.

X-ray diffraction technology uses X-rays to take photographic images of atomic particles. It's called X-ray crystallography when it's used to record the positions of atoms inside crystals such as salt crystals, diamond crystals, or protein crystals.

By taking two completely different routes, both Francis Crick and James Watson *(left to right)* somehow wound up at the Cavendish Laboratory in 1951. While Watson's interest lay in zoology and Crick's in physics, by 1951, both men had switched to the emerging field of molecular biology. They came from different worlds and had extremely different personalities, but their partnership worked and would forever change modern science. Immediately after they first met, Watson, then twenty-three, and Crick, thirty-five, decided to team up and solve the century's greatest mystery: the structure of DNA. The two were driven, mostly by their own passion and dedication but also by several other scientists who were also determined to find the answer to DNA first. This photo captures the duo in Cambridge in 1953, shortly before their remarkable discovery.

how genes work. The book changed the course of Watson's life. He became absolutely determined to unlock the secret of the gene.

## Changing Countries

After getting his degree in zoology from the University of Chicago, Watson attended Indiana University and obtained his

## BACTERIA VS. VIRUSES

A bacterium is a microscopic, single-celled organism. A virus is a microscopic organism consisting mostly of nucleic acid inside a coating of protein. A bacterium is self-replicating, meaning that it can reproduce itself. A virus invades other living cells, such as a bacterium or a human body cell, and uses that cell to reproduce itself.

Ph.D. in zoology in 1950. Watson then went to Copenhagen, Denmark, to work with a biochemist there, but he found he didn't like the work at all.

A turning point came in Naples, Italy, where he heard a talk by Maurice Wilkins, an expert in X-ray crystallography. Wilkins showed a slide of an X-ray diffraction picture of DNA. The image convinced Watson that DNA has a regular structure of some kind. He felt that understanding this structure would give him the answer to the gene.

In 1951, Watson traveled to England and won acceptance into the prestigious Cambridge University from the head of Cavendish Laboratory, Sir Lawrence Bragg. Watson's acceptance into the school meant he was to aid Max Perutz, another X-ray crystallographer, in the study of the structure of hemoglobin. So it was by several unexpected twists of fate that Watson and Crick both found themselves at Cavendish in 1951, a critical time in the race to unlock the secrets of DNA.

# CHAPTER 2

The early 1950s was a fascinating and turbulent time period. The United States' flag contained only forty-eight stars (Hawaii and Alaska weren't admitted as states until 1959). A famous World War II general, "Ike" Eisenhower, was president. Queen Elizabeth II of the United Kingdom had her coronation in June 1953.

## Politics

# THE WORLD OF THE 1950s

The 1950s were also the start of what was called the Cold War, when relations between the United States and the Soviet Union came to a long standoff. While not openly at war, the capitalist United States and the Communist Soviet Union were in a life and death struggle over world politics, ideology, economics, and military strength. For decades, it seemed as though a nuclear war could break out between the two superpowers.

By 1950, America had enjoyed several years basking in the glow of a hard-won victory over Germany and Japan in World War II. But Communism was perceived as a serious threat to the American way of life. As tensions between America and the Soviet Union rose, American public sentiment toward Soviet citizens reached a boiling point. As Communists, the Soviets were dubbed "Reds" for their bold red national flag. Senator Joseph McCarthy capitalized on the

While many think of 1950s America as the time of classic cars and Elvis Presley, the Cold War sent chills through the spine of the nation. The Red Scare, which was essentially a Communist witch hunt, was propagated mainly by Senator Joseph McCarthy *(above center)*. The Wisconsin senator spread fear throughout the land, insisting that Communists were living in America and intent on bringing down the nation. McCarthy, along with his House Un-American Activities Committee (HUAC), sought to find these Communists and bring them to justice. In reality, McCarthy's movement simply fed off paranoia of the Communist Soviet Union. As a result, many innocent people were accused of being Communists during McCarthy's rampage. Eventually, McCarthyism lost momentum as people refocused their concerns on reality. The McCarthy era remains as one of the darkest episodes in American history.

American public's fear of Communists for political gain. He created the so-called Red Scare to make Americans fear that there were "Commies" hiding under every bed. For several years, McCarthy ruthlessly went after anyone who might be a Communist, destroying careers and lives in what many considered a witch hunt.

Also during this time, the Korean War erupted in Southeast Asia. In 1948, Korea had split into two nations, Communist North Korea and anti-Communist South Korea. America backed the South, while the North was supported by the Communist nations of China and the Soviet Union.

## The Baby Boom

Against this backdrop of world struggles, Americans at home were engaged in the first baby boom as thousands of men returned from World War II and started families. There were worries about inflation and labor struggles, but overall America was booming, and popular technology along with it.

The invention of transistors allowed radios to shrink to a handheld size and hearing aids could fit inside an ear. The credit card surged into widespread use for the first time. Denim became fashionable. First-class mail cost three cents. Television was broadcast in black and white, and *I Love Lucy* was the number-one hit show. One of the first computers, UNIVAC, was so big it filled an entire building.

## Atomic Power

In technology, one issue overshadowed all others—atomic power. During World War II, the United States became the first country to use atomic bombs as weapons. The U.S. military dropped two atomic bombs on the Japanese cities of Hiroshima and Nagasaki in August 1945. The bombs ended the war by nearly destroying both cities and killing more than 95,000 people. Less than four years later, the Soviet Union tested its first atomic bomb. The arms race was on.

Following World War II, the Cold War enveloped much of the world in a tenuous arms race that lasted for more than four decades. The standoff was primarily between the United States and the Soviet Union. The United States and its allies in the West wanted to halt the spread of Communism. This would lead directly to both the Korean and Vietnam Wars. While the United States and the Soviet Union built up a massive amount of arms, these two superpowers never came to blows. This photograph, taken in 1963, is of a military parade in Red Square in Moscow, Russia. Because of paranoia and the rapid improvement of technology and weapons, the Cold War reached its peak in the early 1960s, after which it began a steady decline until 1991, when the Soviet Union collapsed.

The United States developed the far more powerful hydrogen bomb (H-bomb) and tested it in November 1952. The Soviets again followed suit by exploding an H-bomb in August 1953.

Americans lived in fear of an atomic war, and children were taught to "duck and cover"—to duck under their desks and cover their heads in case of an atomic attack.

But atomic power was also seen as a potential answer to all energy problems for both civilian and military use as the first nuclear submarine was completed in 1953. At that time, concepts for plants that generate atomic power were in the earliest stages of design. No one had the foresight to worry about the problem of nuclear waste.

## Medicine

In medicine, the key new developments included the discovery of the link between tobacco smoking and lung cancer, and the significant gains made in the fight against tuberculosis (TB).

The most serious epidemic at the time was polio. Polio was raging through America, Canada, Australia, and other parts of the world. The polio virus attacks the central nervous system and causes paralysis. Thousands died and thousands more, many of them children, were left crippled for life.

In 1953, American doctor Jonas Salk earned the gratitude of the world by developing a vaccine against polio. His vaccine saved thousands of lives. Now polio has almost been wiped out around the world.

## Stepping-Stones to DNA

While many focused on the rapidly changing social and political climate of the twentieth century, others turned their genius toward the chase for the secret to life itself. DNA had been identified since 1869, but there were many significant discoveries to follow that would demonstrate the importance of genes and DNA.

Here is a quick sketch of famous scientists who came before Watson and Crick in studying the mysteries of the gene.

Up until the first half of the twentieth century, the world's children were constantly at risk for contracting polio, a deadly disease that attacks the immune system. World leaders—from Roman emperor Claudius to United States president Franklin D. Roosevelt—were stricken, but survived, bouts with polio as children. However, the 1950s witnessed a major breakthrough in the fight against this disease. On February 23, 1954, Jonas Salk administered the first inoculation of children against polio. The disease was virtually stopped in its tracks. Here, Dr. Jonas Salk administers an inoculation to a young girl in Pittsburgh, Pennsylvania, in 1955.

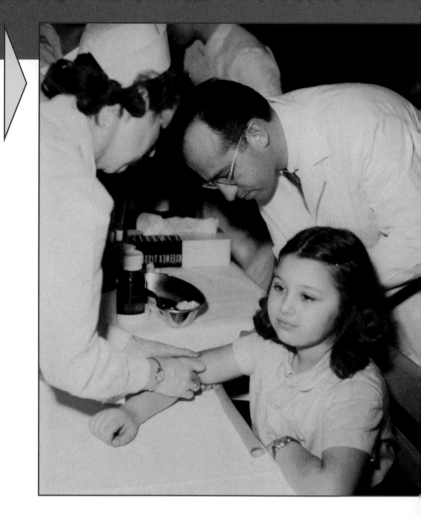

## Gregor Mendel

In 1856, an Austrian monk named Gregor Mendel began experiments growing peas, which resulted in discovering many of the rules by which physical traits are passed on. These became known as the Mendelian laws of inheritance.

## Charles Darwin

In 1859, Charles Darwin published *On the Origin of Species*, in which he made important observations on how physical traits are passed along within species. His book, in particular his theory on how evolution works, stirred up tremendous controversy. Exactly how a species evolves is still being debated and questioned, with modern genetics providing many of the answers.

### Friedrich Miescher

In 1869, a Swiss biochemist named Friedrich Miescher isolated a new molecule, nuclein, from the nucleus of a cell. Though he didn't know it, what he had found was DNA.

### Walther Flemming

In 1882, a German anatomist named Walther Flemming discovered threadlike substances occurring during cell division. These became known as chromosomes. These threadlike structures are made of DNA and protein. They are found in the nuclei of cells.

### Theodor Boveri

Theodor Boveri, a German scientist, began studying chromosomes in 1887. He saw that chromosomes remained the same in the new cells after cell division, and he deduced that they contributed to the inheritance of traits. He determined that a sperm and an egg contribute the same number of chromosomes to the offspring. He also made a great intuitive leap in suggesting that abnormal chromosomes might be responsible for cancerous tumors.

### Thomas Hunt Morgan

In 1933, biologist Thomas Hunt Morgan received a Nobel Prize for his pioneering work in genetics. Starting in 1907, Morgan bred millions of fruit flies and documented how mutant traits were inherited and passed on. He was able to prove that some inherited traits were linked to the sex of the fly (male or female) and that genes located on the chromosomes carried this inheritance information.

## ENZYMES

Enzymes are a type of protein. The job of an enzyme is to provide extra energy to make chemical reactions happen within the cells. Think of an enzyme as providing an extra "jolt" to get a reaction going. There are millions of enzymes, and an organism can't function without them. An example of an enzyme that helps a human body to function is lactase, which allows us to digest milk. Without lactase, milk becomes a poison to us.

### George Beadle and Edward Tatum

In 1941, scientists George Beadle and Edward Tatum proved that genes are responsible for the production of enzymes: the DNA in genes tells the cell what enzyme to make and how to make it.

### Oswald Avery

Oswald Avery, a Canadian-born American biochemist, spent many years studying the dangerous bacterium that causes pneumonia, an inflammation of the lungs. In 1944, his studies proved that transferring DNA from one pneumonia bacterium to another determines how that other bacterium will grow. Therefore, DNA alone had to be the source of the genetic code. Oswald's work helped inspire Watson and Crick to focus on DNA as the unit of genetic inheritance.

# CHAPTER 3

## UPS AND DOWNS

In April 1951, the famous American chemist Linus Pauling and his American colleagues, Robert Corey and Herman Branson, published their findings on what was called the alpha-helix, which forms the backbones of tens of thousands of proteins. After learning of this discovery, the highly competitive but still unknown Watson was determined to arrive at the answer to DNA before Pauling did.

Pauling influenced both Watson and Crick in another critical way. Pauling had built a physical model to work out his discovery. His model looked something like clusters of billiard balls stacked in a coil. Watson and Crick had to resort to simpler materials to build their model for the structure of DNA.

### A Friendship Begins

A few days after arriving in Cambridge in mid-October 1951, Jim Watson met Francis Crick at the Cavendish Laboratory. The two men immediately sparked one another's intellectual brilliance. In *The Double Helix*, Watson says he "immediately discovered the fun of talking to Francis Crick." And Crick, in *What Mad Pursuit*, says, "Jim [Watson] and I hit it off immediately, partly because our interests were astonishingly similar and partly, I suspect, because a certain youthful arrogance, a ruthlessness, and an impatience with sloppy thinking came naturally to both of us."

They were soon sharing meals together at the local pub so they could continue their conversations once work at the lab had ended. At the Cavendish Laboratory, the other scientists gave a vacant office to Watson and Crick so they could talk to one another without disturbing the others. Some of the scientists didn't like Crick's loud laugh and tendency to talk at great length.

## LINUS PAULING

With a career spanning from 1921 to 1994, Pauling was one of the world's most famous chemists and made many significant discoveries. In 1954, he won the Nobel Prize in Chemistry for his work on the structure of protein and antibodies. In 1962, he was awarded the Nobel Peace Prize for helping bring about the Nuclear Test Ban Treaty between the United States and the Soviet Union. The treaty banned nuclear testing.

## Going Against the Grain

When Watson and Crick met that fall, neither one of them had official permission to work on the problem of DNA. There was an unwritten but very powerful code of etiquette in British science that prevented one scientist from competing in an area that officially belonged to another scientist.

Crick was meant to be finishing his Ph.D. thesis on the X-ray diffraction of proteins. Meanwhile, Watson was supposed to be helping Max Perutz crystallize myoglobin (a protein found in muscle cells) to use in X-ray images. But both of their minds were bent on unraveling the mystery of DNA.

## Wilkins and Franklin

Crick was an old friend of Maurice Wilkins's, an expert in X-ray crystallography at the King's College Laboratory in London. Wilkins was officially designated to be working on the DNA problem. At King's, they were attempting to find the structure of DNA by taking X-ray diffraction pictures of protein crystals.

One of the first roadblocks Watson and Crick ran into was a clash of personalities between Wilkins and a newly arrived X-ray crystallographer, Rosalind Franklin. Franklin was a brilliant scientist, but in the male-dominated world of 1950s science, she had a difficult time being accepted and respected as a scientist. In fact, she wasn't even allowed to have coffee in one of the faculty rooms, which was reserved for men only.

Consequently, Franklin was extremely defensive about her position and secretive about her work because she wanted to make sure everything she did was beyond the criticism of her male colleagues. It meant that Watson and Crick weren't able to

Born in New Zealand, Maurice Wilkins *(left)* moved to England at the age of six. He went on to study physics at St. John's in Cambridge. Like Francis Crick, Wilkins used his great mind to aid the war effort during World War II by improving radar screens used by the military. Following the war, he turned to biophysics, which would soon lead him to Watson and Crick. In 1962, the three would share the Nobel Prize in Physiology or Medicine. Rosalind Franklin *(right)* would also play an integral role in the Watson-Crick model for DNA. It was her X-ray of a DNA strand, known as photo 51, that would be the ultimate clue Watson and Crick needed. Possibly because of her gender, Franklin never quite received proper recognition for her role in solving the mystery of DNA. And sadly, she never realized the true importance of her work. She died of cancer in 1958, at the age of thirty-seven.

see the new X-ray photos that Franklin was achieving until she was ready to show them.

## Franklin's Pictures

In November 1951, Watson went to London to hear Wilkins and Franklin speak about their work. Franklin showed slides of two

## THE CLUES

Watson and Crick decided to start building some physical models. They felt that putting a model together would help them work out the structure of DNA in a short time. In order to accomplish this, Watson and Crick relied upon several pieces of established information:

- They knew that DNA had to have a "backbone" and that this backbone was made of a combination of sugar-phosphate atoms. But they didn't know whether this backbone ran down the middle or was on the outside of the structure.

- They learned from Wilkins that the thick diameter of DNA on the X-ray photos meant it had to consist of more than one chain of sugar-phosphate backbones. The trouble was that it might be anywhere from two to 100 chains.

- There are four established chemical bases that are the prime components of DNA. The four bases are adenine, guanine, thymine, and cytosine. They are referred to by their first initials as A, G, T, and C. What no one knew yet was how these four bases fit onto the sugar-phosphate backbone or how they functioned to carry genetic information.

forms of protein crystal X-ray photos: the A, or "dry" form, and the B, or "wet" form. When protein crystals dried out in the A form, they contracted into tight, jumbled forms. The B form, which held more water, was harder to achieve but gave a simpler and more revealing photo.

Unfortunately, Watson didn't take notes and didn't yet know much about X-ray crystallography. Therefore, the information he gave to Crick upon his return to Cambridge wasn't entirely accurate. Crick deduced that their choices were narrowed down to a two-, three-, or four-part sugar-phosphate chain.

They also needed other information, which they found by poring over a book by Pauling entitled *The Nature of the Chemical Bond*. They used Pauling's book so much that they had to buy two copies, one for each of them.

## The First Model

Having narrowed down the number of possible chains, Watson and Crick were ready to start experimenting with their model, but first they needed the parts to build it. They took some models they had of carbon atoms, and Watson added bits of copper wire that would represent the larger-sized phosphorus atoms.

Based on the slightly faulty information from Watson's memory, the two built their first model consisting of three chains in a triple helix with the phosphates on the inside of the structure. Wilkins and Franklin soon traveled to Cambridge to see it, but Franklin gave them a devastating critique, pointing out everything they'd gotten wrong.

Worse yet, head of the Cavendish, Sir Lawrence Bragg, discovered what was going on and ordered Watson and Crick to confine themselves to the work they were supposed to be doing. By the end of 1951, it looked as though Watson and Crick's work on DNA was ending before it even began.

## Laying Low

For the first half of 1952, Watson and Crick decided to lay low to appease Bragg. They also needed new data before they could make another attempt at creating an accurate DNA model. They continued to read Pauling's book and do quiet study, but they had to restrict their discussions of DNA to their lunch hours at the Eagle, the local pub.

## Chargaff's Rule

In 1952, Watson and Crick came across another piece to the puzzle. This came through the virtue of studies done by Austrian bio-chemist Erwin Chargaff. Chargaff and his students did many painstaking analyses of DNA samples and found that there was nearly always the same amount of adenine (A) as there was thymine (T), and the same amount of guanine (G) as there was cytosine (C). This became known as Chargaff's rule.

## A Lull in the Action

Summer came and went with no advances. In September 1952, Linus Pauling's son, Peter, arrived to work at the Cavendish Laboratory and shared offices with Watson and Crick. Watson, Crick, and Peter Pauling quickly became friends. This friendship also allowed Watson and Crick to learn news about what Linus Pauling was doing with his research.

In December 1952, Watson and Crick's spirits hit an all-time low. Peter Pauling received a letter from his famous father stating that he had figured out a structure for DNA. It looked as though Watson and Crick's dream was over.

## The Race Is On

Watson and Crick waited several months for some dramatic announcement by Pauling. As 1952 turned into 1953, Rosalind Franklin also announced a change—she was leaving King's and giving up her study of DNA. In turn, Wilkins announced he would return to his study of DNA as soon as Franklin left.

American physicist Linus Pauling thought he was on the right track to solving the mystery of DNA. And he was very close. During World War II, he was heavily involved in political activism. During the McCarthy era that followed, Pauling was labeled a Communist and his travels were restricted. This had a serious effect on a scientist who constantly needed to travel the world in search of the structure of DNA. If he had been able to get to England and meet with Watson and Crick, he would have known that his models for DNA were way off. This page is taken from one of Linus Pauling's notebooks, which contains handwritten notes about the construction of nucleic acids. (See page 56 for a transcription.)

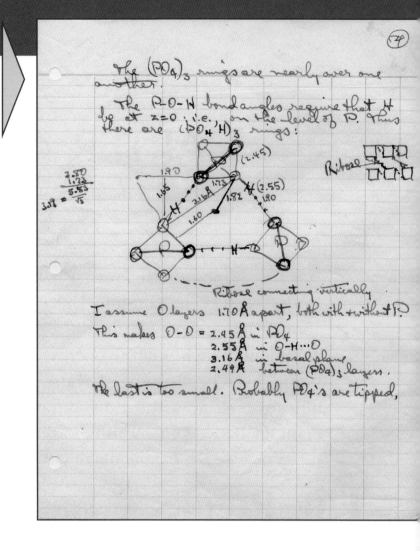

In January 1953, Watson obtained an advance copy of Pauling's paper on the structure of DNA from Peter Pauling. The elder Pauling had decided upon a three-chain helix with the sugar-phosphate backbones in the center.

Watson and Crick instantly knew that Pauling's structure was wrong. They also knew that as soon as the paper was published, Pauling would learn of his mistakes and probably turn around to find the right solution. The publication date was only six weeks away.

The race was on. Watson and Crick plunged back into the problem with renewed energy. They had just six weeks to find the answer.

# CHAPTER 4

## THE PIECES COME TOGETHER

In that same month, January 1953, Watson once again visited King's College in London. There, he tried to talk to Franklin about Pauling's paper, but the two ended up having a terrible argument, which Wilkins overheard. Afterward, in a moment of sympathy, Wilkins showed Watson something of profound significance—it was the now-famous photo 51, an X-ray photo Franklin had taken months earlier. It was a B form photo of excellent detail showing the structure of a DNA molecule.

In *The Double Helix*, Watson writes, "The instant I saw the picture my mouth fell open and my pulse began to race. The pattern was unbelievably simpler than those obtained previously. Moreover, the black cross of reflections which dominated the picture could arise only from a helical structure."

On the train back to Cambridge, Watson sketched out the image as best he could remember it on the margin of a newspaper. Based on the pattern he had seen, he decided on a two-chain concept.

### Permission Granted

Watson immediately went to Sir Lawrence Bragg and convinced Bragg that the Cavendish lab should try to beat Pauling to the

Rosalind Franklin's photo 51 would be the missing piece in the DNA puzzle for Watson and Crick. Franklin used a technique called X-ray diffraction to capture a DNA image for the first time. In this process, the X-rays are so short they actually bounce off the DNA's atoms. The X-rays then scatter, or defract, in different directions. As the X-rays leave the DNA, they leave behind a pattern that photographic film can capture. The "X" pattern at the center of this photograph was what Watson saw that turned on a light in his mind. That very pattern would become the double helix and finally solve the riddle of DNA.

punch. Bragg authorized Watson to start building models again, and Watson did so in earnest.

Crick wasn't ready to accept a two-chain concept just yet. He wanted them to keep open minds as they worked on the models. But when some of the parts arrived a few days later, Watson immediately began experimenting with a two-chain model with the sugar-phosphate backbone on the inside.

By early 1953, the race to unravel the mysteries of DNA was reaching its finish. Watson and Crick's article "Molecular Structure of Nucleic Acids" appeared in *Nature* magazine on April 25, 1953. Following its publication, the duo was propelled to worldwide fame. This photo captures Crick *(left)* and Watson shortly after the publication of their article. The article begins, "This structure has novel features which are of considerable biological interest." These words would become a monumental understatement. Understanding the structure of DNA has helped scientists unravel some of the secrets of life itself and is widely regarded as one of the most important scientific discoveries of all time.

## Back to Model Building

Since he was still waiting for some parts he needed to build his model, and because he had nothing to lose, Watson began building a different version of the model with the backbone on the outside of the molecule. At first, Watson thought that the pairing of bases was like-to-like. That would mean that A would always pair to A, and G would always pair to G, C to C, and T to T.

Jerry Donohue, a visiting American crystallographer, helped with another important piece of information. Watson and Crick were using forms of the four bases that were commonly found in textbooks. Donohue pointed out that new research said those forms were wrong, and he gave Watson the new forms that he should be using. The small but vital changes in the shapes of the bases made a big difference in how the model should be put together. This information instantly dismissed Watson's like-to-like theory. Furthermore, Crick kept insisting that they had to keep Chargaff's rule in mind. Crick was convinced that Chargaff's rule was a key to the answer

## The Answer Is Found

By late February, the new parts had not arrived. Impatient with waiting, Watson cut out cardboard pieces to use until the metal parts were ready. On February 28, 1953, Watson cleared a space off his desk and began playing around with his cardboard pieces. He looked up for a minute when Donohue entered the office, thinking it was Crick.

When he looked back down, his eye fell on a certain combination of the cardboard pieces. In *The Double Helix*, he relates the moment when he suddenly "became aware that an adenine-thymine pair held together by two hydrogen bonds was identical in shape to a guanine-cystosine pair held together by at least two hydrogen bonds." The combination of A=T and G=C immediately brought to mind Chargaff's rule. This was it!

Crick was only halfway through the door when Watson told him they'd found the answer. Though Crick was cautious at first, remembering their previous mistakes, it took him only a few minutes to see that this model worked. Not only did it give them

No. 4356  April 25, 1953     NATURE     737

equipment, and to Dr. G. E. R. Deacon and the captain and officers of R.R.S. *Discovery II* for their part in making the observations.

[1] Young, F. B., Gerrard, H., and Jevons, W., *Phil. Mag.*, **40**, 149 (1920).
[2] Longuet-Higgins, M. S., *Mon. Not. Roy. Astro. Soc., Geophys. Supp.*, **5**, 285 (1949).
[3] Von Arx, W. S., *Woods Hole Papers in Phys. Ocearog. Meteor.*, **11** (3) (1950).
[4] Ekman, V. W., *Arkiv. Mat. Astron. Fysik. (Stockholm)*, **2** (11) (1905).

## MOLECULAR STRUCTURE OF NUCLEIC ACIDS

### A Structure for Deoxyribose Nucleic Acid

WE wish to suggest a structure for the salt of deoxyribose nucleic acid (D.N.A.). This structure has novel features which are of considerable biological interest.

A structure for nucleic acid has already been proposed by Pauling and Corey[1]. They kindly made their manuscript available to us in advance of publication. Their model consists of three inter-twined chains, with the phosphates near the fibre axis, and the bases on the outside. In our opinion, this structure is unsatisfactory for two reasons: (1) We believe that the material which gives the X-ray diagrams is the salt, not the free acid. Without the acidic hydrogen atoms it is not clear what forces would hold the structure together, especially as the negatively charged phosphates near the axis will repel each other. (2) Some of the van der Waals distances appear to be too small.

Another three-chain structure has also been suggested by Fraser (in the press). In his model the phosphates are on the outside and the bases on the inside, linked together by hydrogen bonds. This structure as described is rather ill-defined, and for this reason we shall not comment on it.

We wish to put forward a radically different structure for the salt of deoxyribose nucleic acid. This structure has two helical chains each coiled round the same axis (see diagram). We have made the usual chemical assumptions, namely, that each chain consists of phosphate di-ester groups joining β-D-deoxy-ribofuranose residues with 3',5' linkages. The two chains (but not their bases) are related by a dyad perpendicular to the fibre axis. Both chains follow right-handed helices, but owing to the dyad the sequences of the atoms in the two chains run in opposite directions. Each chain loosely resembles Furberg's[2] model No. 1; that is, the bases are on the inside of the helix and the phosphates on the outside. The configuration of the sugar and the atoms near it is close to Furberg's 'standard configuration', the sugar being roughly perpendicular to the attached base. There

is a residue on each chain every 3·4 A. in the z-direction. We have assumed an angle of 36° between adjacent residues in the same chain, so that the structure repeats after 10 residues on each chain, that is, after 34 A. The distance of a phosphorus atom from the fibre axis is 10 A. As the phosphates are on the outside, cations have easy access to them.

The structure is an open one, and its water content is rather high. At lower water contents we would expect the bases to tilt so that the structure could become more compact.

The novel feature of the structure is the manner in which the two chains are held together by the purine and pyrimidine bases. The planes of the bases are perpendicular to the fibre axis. They are joined together in pairs, a single base from one chain being hydrogen-bonded to a single base from the other chain, so that the two lie side by side with identical z-co-ordinates. One of the pair must be a purine and the other a pyrimidine for bonding to occur. The hydrogen bonds are made as follows: purine position 1 to pyrimidine position 1; purine position 6 to pyrimidine position 6.

If it is assumed that the bases only occur in the structure in the most plausible tautomeric forms (that is, with the keto rather than the enol configurations) it is found that only specific pairs of bases can bond together. These pairs are: adenine (purine) with thymine (pyrimidine), and guanine (purine) with cytosine (pyrimidine).

In other words, if an adenine forms one member of a pair, on either chain, then on these assumptions the other member must be thymine; similarly for guanine and cytosine. The sequence of bases on a single chain does not appear to be restricted in any way. However, if only specific pairs of bases can be formed, it follows that if the sequence of bases on one chain is given, then the sequence on the other chain is automatically determined.

It has been found experimentally[3,4] that the ratio of the amounts of adenine to thymine, and the ratio of guanine to cytosine, are always very close to unity for deoxyribose nucleic acid.

It is probably impossible to build this structure with a ribose sugar in place of the deoxyribose, as the extra oxygen atom would make too close a van der Waals contact.

The previously published X-ray data[5,6] on deoxyribose nucleic acid are insufficient for a rigorous test of our structure. So far as we can tell, it is roughly compatible with the experimental data, but it must be regarded as unproved until it has been checked against more exact results. Some of these are given in the following communications. We were not aware of the details of the results presented there when we devised our structure, which rests mainly though not entirely on published experimental data and stereo-chemical arguments.

It has not escaped our notice that the specific pairing we have postulated immediately suggests a possible copying mechanism for the genetic material.

Full details of the structure, including the conditions assumed in building it, together with a set of co-ordinates for the atoms, will be published elsewhere.

We are much indebted to Dr. Jerry Donohue for constant advice and criticism, especially on inter-atomic distances. We have also been stimulated by a knowledge of the general nature of the unpublished experimental results and ideas of Dr. M. H. F. Wilkins, Dr. R. E. Franklin and their co-workers at

This figure is purely diagrammatic. The two ribbons symbolize the two phosphate—sugar chains, and the horizontal rods the pairs of bases holding the chains together. The vertical line marks the fibre axis

Solving the structure of DNA took years and the work of many brilliant minds, each of which helped each other along the way. In the end, it was a race to the finish to see who could come up with the correct structure of DNA. A month following their ground-breaking article, "Molecular Structure of Nucleic Acids," Watson and Crick again turned to *Nature* and published "Genetical Implications of the Structure of Deoxyribonucleic Acid." In it, Watson and Crick explain how base pairing in the double helix allows replication of DNA. These are some of the handwritten notes by Francis Crick for the manuscript of that second monumental article.

a double helix with shape and measurements that fit the known data, it also gave them a mechanism for a genetic code that could easily create a template and reproduce itself. The only thing that remained was to get the proper metal parts to build a real model and confirm their find.

## Dramatic Announcements

All the same, in *The Double Helix*, Watson relates, "I felt slightly queasy when at lunch Francis winged into The Eagle to tell everyone within hearing distance that we had found the secret of life."

Crick also gave the news to his wife, Odile, at dinner. Years later, Odile confessed she hadn't believed him because he was always coming home and saying things like that.

The article "Genetical Implications of the Structure of Deoxyribonucleic Acid" appeared in *Nature* on May 30, 1953, as a follow-up piece to "Molecular Structure of Nucleic Acids." The discovery of the structure of DNA was by no means instantly hailed as a success. It took the work of several others to validate Watson and Crick's findings. Even Linus Pauling clung to his erroneous findings during this time. By the end of the 1950s, there was no arguing that Watson and Crick's structure was correct. By then, biology laboratories around the world had begun implementing the new structure of DNA. This is the first page of Watson and Crick's second *Nature* article. (See page 56 for a transcription.)

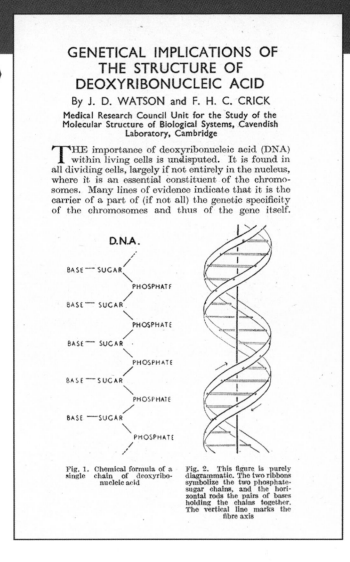

## GENETICAL IMPLICATIONS OF THE STRUCTURE OF DEOXYRIBONUCLEIC ACID

By J. D. WATSON and F. H. C. CRICK

Medical Research Council Unit for the Study of the Molecular Structure of Biological Systems, Cavendish Laboratory, Cambridge

THE importance of deoxyribonucleic acid (DNA) within living cells is undisputed. It is found in all dividing cells, largely if not entirely in the nucleus, where it is an essential constituent of the chromosomes. Many lines of evidence indicate that it is the carrier of a part of (if not all) the genetic specificity of the chromosomes and thus of the gene itself.

Fig. 1. Chemical formula of a single chain of deoxyribonucleic acid

Fig. 2. This figure is purely diagrammatic. The two ribbons symbolize the two phosphate-sugar chains, and the horizontal rods the pairs of bases holding the chains together. The vertical line marks the fibre axis

The next day, Watson managed to finally get the parts from the machine shop. Since only one person at a time could work on the model, Watson put the first arrangements together with Crick checking it afterward. The final model featured ten base pairs and was six feet (two meters) high.

During that week, Wilkins saw the model and checked Watson and Crick's measurements against his own data. Franklin also agreed that their data supported the model. It was agreed that Wilkins and his X-ray team, plus Franklin and her lab partner, Raymond Gosling, would write their papers about their X-ray results to go out at the same time as the paper Watson and Crick would write about their DNA discovery. This was both a matter of professional courtesy and because the X-ray pictures were an important proof to back up the discovery.

Watson wanted to be cautious about what they put in the paper, but Crick insisted on one line indicating that they had realized the potential of the double-helix structure to be self-replicating. That line reads, "It has not escaped our notice that the specific pairing we have postulated immediately suggests a possible copying mechanism for the genetic material." This was possibly the understatement of the century.

Bragg approved the paper, and it was sent to the prestigious scientific journal *Nature* to be accepted for publication. On April 25, 1953, the article appeared entitled "A Structure for Deoxyribose Nucleic Acid." The authors flipped a coin to see whose name would come first. That's why the byline read Watson and Crick, rather than Crick and Watson.

The news hit the scientific world with a big splash. Even before the article came out, Linus Pauling heard about the discovery and came to Cambridge to see the model for himself. He graciously agreed that Watson and Crick had found the answer.

Five weeks later, Watson and Crick followed up with a second article in *Nature*, in which they speculated further about the genetic implications of their discovery. Watson was only twenty-five, Crick was thirty-six, and already their names were firmly established in scientific history. They had truly found the secret of life.

# CHAPTER 5

**M**uch more about DNA has been learned since 1953. It is a very complicated subject with new discoveries being made all the time. However, certain basics are now well-known and we will cover those.

As you have learned in basic biology classes, our bodies are made up of trillions of cells. The cells are specialized to become skin, hair, or teeth, or to form organs such as the liver, heart, or brain.

## THE BASICS OF DNA

A cell is enclosed by a membrane. Inside that membrane is the jellylike cytoplasm and the nucleus. The cytoplasm contains organelles (small "organs" that serve various functions such as creating proteins). The nucleus is the command center of the cell.

Inside the nucleus of every cell, there is DNA, which contains our entire genetic code. All of this genetic material inside the nucleus is known as the genome. The genome consists of pairs of chromosomes, which contain genes, which are made of DNA.

### The Genetic Code

Crick referred to DNA as a very long chemical message written in a four-letter language, in which the genome is the entire book of instructions for your body, chromosomes are the chapters of

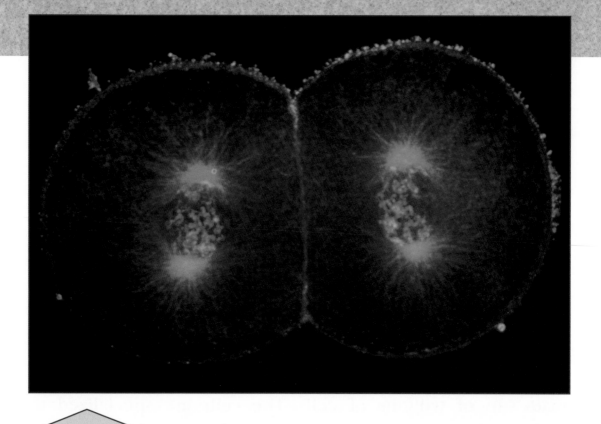

Here is a magnified photograph of a fertilized sea urchin embryo dividing from one parent cell into two daughter cells. The cell is in the process of mitosis, when the nucleus divides into two identical cells. The cells' chromosomes *(blue)* have condensed and are beginning to align at the middle of the cell. Next, the chromosomes will separate at their sister chromatids, which contain genetic information. This will allow for one cell to divide into two identical cells. The two new daughter cells are identical to each other and to the original parent cell.

the book, genes are the sentences of each chapter, and DNA is the individual letters that make up the words.

## The Genome

The genome is the complete set of instructions for re-creating the organism. Each organism can be identified by its genome. A human genome is different from a cat genome or a flower genome. Yet every single organism has tiny variations within the genome that make each individual genome unique. This means that no two humans have precisely the same genome. There is more genetic difference between a tall person and a short one than between white skin and black skin. Those tiny, tiny variations are why humans look different from one another.

At the same time, even though a human being can be male or female, be tall or short, have blue or green or brown eyes, our genomes are 99.9 percent the same. That's why we can identify a common human genome for all human beings.

## Chromosomes

The genome consists of chromosomes, which are threadlike structures found in the nucleus of the cell. Chromosomes are made of DNA and protein. DNA molecules are extremely long and thin, so the protein provides a "scaffolding" to hold the DNA in an organized shape. The DNA coils around the protein, which keeps it in a compact form and protects the DNA from damage. It is somewhat similar to wrapping thread around a spool to keep the thread from tangling or breaking until it's needed.

Chromosomes come in pairs. Humans have forty-six chromosomes. In humans, an egg and a sperm cell each carries half of the mother's or father's chromosomes: twenty-three in the egg and twenty-three in the sperm. When the two cells come together, the twenty-three chromosomes form the complete set of forty-six, and in this way, each of us inherits characteristics from both of our parents.

## Genes

Each chromosome in a human cell contains from a few hundred to a few thousand genes. Genes (the "sentences" of the genetic code) are specific sections of DNA that are located on the chromosomes. One gene can determine a certain characteristic,

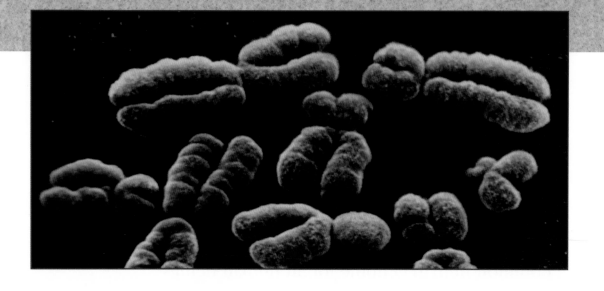

This photograph is a color-enhanced scanning electron micrograph of human chromosomes. Chromosomes are formed from the intertwined molecules of DNA found in the nucleus of the cell. Humans have forty-six chromosomes, two sets of twenty-three, one from each parent.

though characteristics are usually determined through a combination of genes. One set of genes might determine the color of our eyes, while other genes might determine whether our hair will be straight or curly. Human beings have somewhere around 30,000 genes.

## DNA: The Double Helix

One of the most significant parts of Watson and Crick's historic discovery was recognizing that DNA's structure is the double helix. If you were to take a long, thin strip of paper and twist it in a spiral, you would create a single helix. If you were to take a ladder and twist it into a spiral, that would be a double helix. In fact, DNA looks like a ladder twisted in a spiral.

On this twisted ladder is where the genetic code (made up of the individual "letters") is found. As Crick said, the genetic code is "written" in a long sequence of four letters representing four chemical bases. Those bases are:

A (adenine)
G (guanine)
T (thymine)
C (cytosine)

Each base is connected to a sugar molecule that is connected to a phosphate molecule. This three-part unit is known as a nucleotide. The sugar-phosphate parts of the nucleotide link up to one another to form the two sides of the ladder. The A, G, T,

## CHROMOSOMES IN ORGANISMS

The number of chromosome pairs varies from organism to organism. Here are some examples:

Mosquito: 6

Onion: 16

Cat: 38

Human: 46

Dog: 78

Goldfish: 94

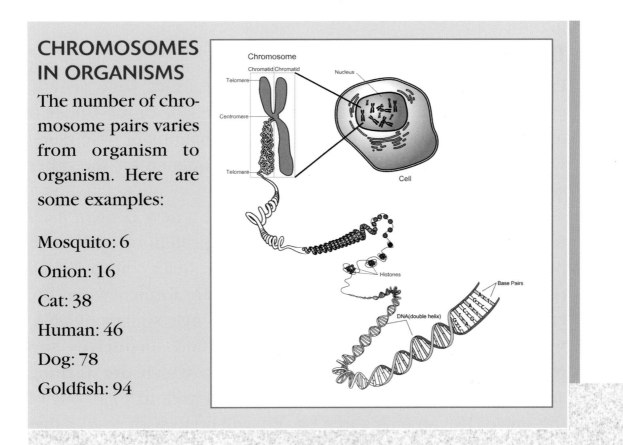

WATSON AND CRICK AND DNA

and C bases in the nucleotides form the rungs of the ladder. Two bases meet in the middle and bond together to create one rung.

If one side of the rung is A, the other side will always be T. If one side of the rung is G, the other side will always be C.

There are four possible combinations of base pairs that make up these rungs (the "=" denotes the bond between the base pairs):

A=T
T=A
G=C
C=G

A single human gene can contain anywhere from 27,000 to 2 million of these base pairs.

## Divide and Conquer

Each side of the DNA ladder contains the exact same genetic code. If a piece of the genetic code on one side of the ladder is AGTCAG, using the above possible combinations of base pairs, we see that there is only one possible sequence for the other side of that same piece: TCAGTC.

When the time comes for a cell to make a new copy of itself (either to replicate itself or to generate a protein or enzyme to perform some function), the DNA double helix "unzips" itself right down the middle of the rungs that are formed when the base pairs bond with each other. The two single strands of DNA, which both have unpaired bases now, find themselves surrounded by free, unattached nucleotides, which are floating around in the cell. A free bit of A will attach itself to a T of one of the single DNA strands; a free bit of T will bond with an A of that strand; a free G will attach to a C of the single strand; and so on.

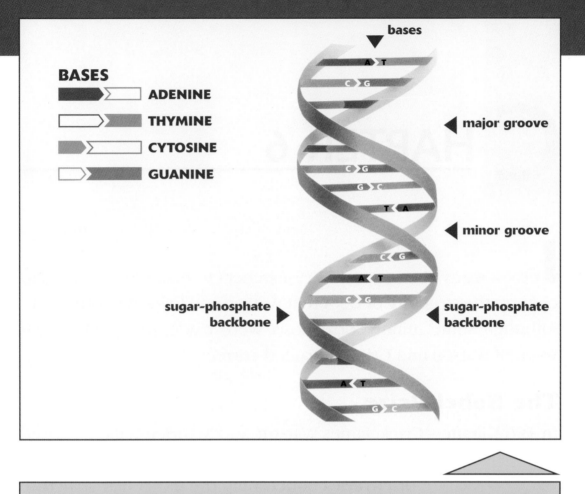

**BASES**
- ADENINE
- THYMINE
- CYTOSINE
- GUANINE

bases

major groove

minor groove

sugar-phosphate backbone ▶

◀ sugar-phosphate backbone

This diagram of the DNA double helix shows its basic structural properties. Paired bases form rungs connecting the two backbones, which are made when the sugar and phosphate attached to a base bond with those of another base. As the backbones twist to form the double helix, the path they take forms a series of major (wider) and minor (narrower) grooves.

Each new base pairing bonds to form a new rung, the sugar and the phosphate attached to each base bond with the sugar and the phosphate of the base on the rungs directly below and directly above it to form the new side of the ladder, and a new complete DNA double helix is formed, with the exact same genetic code as the original one. In fact, two new double helixes have been formed, one from each single "unzipped" strand.

That is how the genetic code is replicated trillions of times to create trillions of new cells. And that is how you began as a single set of chromosomes that became a baby that became the person you are now.

# CHAPTER 6

It took many years for other researchers to make further tests to confirm the structure of DNA that Watson and Crick had proposed. Although some minor corrections were made, the fundamental work of Watson and Crick remained correct.

## The Nobel Prize

In 1962, Francis Crick, James Watson, and Maurice Wilkins shared the Nobel Prize in Physiology or Medicine "for their discoveries concerning the molecular structure of nucleic acids and its significance for information transfer in living material," as cited by the Nobel Foundation.

**THE YEARS THAT FOLLOWED**

Wilkins shared the prize with Watson and Crick because the X-ray crystallography pictures were a vital part of making the discovery. Tragically, Dr. Rosalind Franklin, whose contributions were so important, had died of cancer in 1958, when she was only thirty-seven. Had she lived, she might very well have shared the Nobel Prize with the three men, but the prize is only awarded to living scientists. Many years later, in 2003, the Royal Society, a national academy of science in the UK, established an award fund in Dr. Franklin's name: The Royal Society Rosalind Franklin Award, which honors research that promotes women in science, engineering, and technology.

# A Few Words from Jim Watson

Watson was chosen to deliver the Nobel acceptance speech on December 10, 1962. In his speech, Watson demonstrated his tendency to be very honest about people (including himself), his sense of humor, and his understanding that science doesn't

## THE LEGACY OF ALFRED NOBEL

The Nobel Prize was established in 1901, thanks to Alfred Nobel, a Swedish scientist who invented dynamite. In his will, he left money to establish prizes for major discoveries in science, excellence in literature, and contributions to peace. Experts from Sweden and around the world form committees each year to select the winners. Each year, the highly prestigious awards are given out in Stockholm, Sweden, on December 10, the anniversary of Nobel's death.

*At the Nobel ceremonies in 1962, Watson (second from right) shared the honor with Crick (third from left). Also pictured are Maurice Wilkins (far left), Max Perutz (second from left), John Kendrew (far right), and author John Steinbeck (third from right).*

happen by itself. Watson spoke of science as the output of flawed human beings who strive to find truth. After acknowledging that he never could have discovered the structure of DNA without Crick and Wilkins, he finished his speech like this:

*The last thing I would like to say is that good science as a way of life is sometimes difficult. It often is hard to have confidence that you really know where the future lies. We must thus believe strongly in our ideas, often to point where they may seem tiresome and bothersome and even arrogant to our colleagues. I knew many people, at least when I was young, who thought I was quite unbearable. Some also thought Maurice was very strange, and others, including myself, thought that Francis was at times difficult. Fortunately we were working among wise and tolerant people who understood the spirit of scientific discovery and the conditions necessary for its generation. I feel that it is very important, especially for us so singularly honored, to remember that science does not stand by itself, but is the creation of very human people.*

## The Double-Helix Team Divides

Although they did work together again briefly, Watson and Crick soon took separate paths. Watson helped build a strong school of molecular biology at Harvard University in Cambridge, Massachusetts. In 1968, he married Elizabeth Lewis and they had two children. Also in 1968, he became the director of Cold Spring Harbor Laboratory in New York, of which he later became president. Watson was also instrumental in starting the Human Genome Project and was director of the project from 1989 to 1992.

Following their work on the double helix, Watson *(right)* and Crick *(left)* went their separate ways but remained friends. In 1989, Watson was named head of the Human Genome Project at the National Institutes of Health. The project's ultimate goal was to identify every human gene and analyze how disease affects each one. Watson left the project after just a few years and went on to become president of the laboratory at Cold Spring Harbor, New York. In 1976, Crick moved to San Diego, California, to become part of the Salk Institute for Biological Studies. On July 28, 2004, Francis Crick passed away after a long battle with colon cancer at his home in San Diego.

Crick focused on the relationship between DNA and proteins, which he pursued for many years, and made significant discoveries. In 1976, he went to work at the Salk Institute for Biological Studies in San Diego, California. He stayed in San Diego for the rest of his life. On July 28, 2004, he died at age eighty-eight from colon cancer.

# CHAPTER 7

One of the most significant endeavors in the history of science was the Human Genome Project. Publicly funded with international support, the project was officially launched in 1990, with the purpose of learning the complete sequence of human DNA. Determining the entire sequence of the human genetic code is a vital first step to fully understanding how our genes work. That understanding can be put to many uses, such as preventing and curing disease.

## HOW DNA IS USED TODAY

On April 15, 2003, the project announced that it had completed its work, nearly fifty years from the day Watson and Crick announced their discovery of the double helix.

However, knowing the basic sequence (the order of the genetic "letters") is only a starting point. It's like being presented with the alphabet to an ancient language that no one knows how to read. To understand what it says, one must learn what the words and sentences mean, how the grammar works, and what the final message is. That is why the Human Genome Project was both a monumental achievement and only the beginning of a larger and more complex process of discovery.

Other genomes have also been sequenced in the meantime, such as those of mice, flies, frogs, viruses, bacteria, and some plants.

One direct result of Watson and Crick's work was the creation of the Human Genome Project. This enormous project was aimed at characterizing all known human genetic material by mapping out the complete sequence of DNA in the human genome. The project reached its goal in April 2003, more than two years ahead of schedule. Over the course of the project, an international team mapped out more than 3 billion DNA letters in the human genome.

## Medicine

If there is any one area where studying the genetic code holds crucial promise, it's the field of medicine. As we learn more about what various genes do, we can discover what gene or genes might cause a disease. In 1989, scientists found a single gene that is responsible for cystic fibrosis. Perhaps one day, it will be possible to fix that disease-causing gene before a baby is born.

Better yet, with advancing techniques in gene therapy, it's possible to cure the malfunctioning gene itself. This was the case in

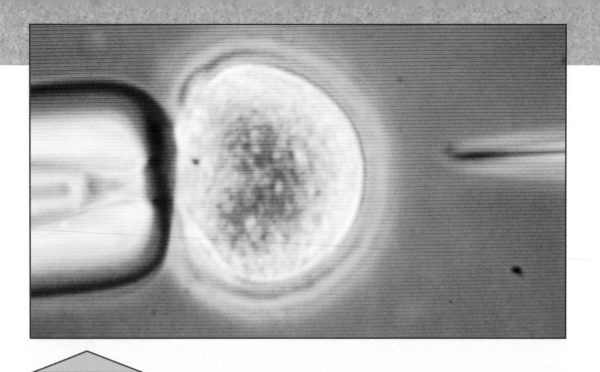

While the mapping of DNA's structure has led to many breakthroughs in the struggle against disease, genetic manipulation remains a hotly contested debate. The study of DNA has sparked many arguments as to how far science should go. For the sake of stopping and curing diseases, should science alter genetic material that occurs naturally? The questions are simple enough, but there are no simple answers. Here, a cell is injected with foreign or increased amounts of DNA.

1990, when a girl was cured of an inherited immune deficiency disorder. Gene therapy is complex because it is rarely only one gene that is the problem. There is much to be learned about how our 30,000 genes work in combination with one another.

## Genetic Engineering

Genetic engineering is a new field filled with many moral questions about what is right and wrong. How far should humans go in altering the genetic code of another living organism?

There are great potential benefits, a lot of them with the food we eat. For example, "golden rice," a form of rice that has been genetically engineered to contain vitamin A, could help millions of people live healthier lives.

Can the same be said of fish that glow in the dark? Using a technique called recombinant DNA, some scientists have inserted genes from one type of organism, such as a fluorescent protein from jellyfish, into the genes of another organism, such as fish, to make it glow.

Cloning, in which the genetic code of one organism is entirely re-created, is another area with tremendous potential for good or bad. The first mammal to be cloned was Dolly the sheep in 1996, at the Roslin Institute in Scotland. She was an exact duplicate of the sheep whose DNA was used. However, there are indications that clones may not live as long and may suffer unforeseen problems. Dolly had to be put to sleep when she was only six years old, after she developed a lung disease. There are ethical questions about creating this kind of life.

On the other side of the scale, cloning could save a species from extinction or provide the means to create organs, such as hearts or livers, that are desperately needed for transplants. Cloning of a type of cell called a stem cell (an undifferentiated cell that can become a specific cell, such as a liver, lung, or heart cell) could provide the means to cure many diseases.

## Engineering Our Food

Today, there is hot debate over the advances of genetically modified plants and food. Genetic techniques can create plants that thrive in salty conditions where most plants couldn't survive or create produce that lasts longer on store shelves.

But there are many questions about how such plants can negatively affect natural plants and change the balance of nature, or what effect they could have on our bodies.

# Crime

The use of genetic "fingerprinting" is one of the success stories of DNA research. A detective can find a tiny drop of blood or a single hair at a crime scene and send it to a genetic lab where the genetic code will be extracted and used to identify whom the DNA came from.

DNA evidence is now used not only to track down the criminals who commit crimes but also to free innocent people who were wrongly convicted. People sentenced to death have been proven not guilty and freed thanks to DNA evidence. Likewise, many criminals who would have gotten away with their crimes have been convicted, thanks to DNA evidence.

## Our Ancestors and Descendants

We can use DNA to track the history of the human race going back thousands and thousands of years. We can also use it to learn who someone's biological parent is or who someone is related to in the present or from the past. In the 1990s, DNA provided evidence that Thomas Jefferson had African American descendants, something that had long been suspected but never proven.

One surprise discovery through DNA research is that about 75,000 years ago, the human race was brought to the brink of extinction by an unknown catastrophe. Perhaps only several thousand people were left alive. From those several thousand people have come every living person on the planet today. This is why we are 99.9 percent the same at the genetic level. It shows us that we really are all related at the most fundamental point of creation—our DNA.

# TIMELINE

| | |
|---|---|
| **June 8, 1916** | — Francis Crick is born in Northampton, England. |
| **April 6, 1928** | — James Watson is born in Chicago, Illinois. |
| **1937** | — Crick graduates from University College, London. |
| **1939** | — Crick goes to work for the British Admiralty helping to design naval weapons. |
| **1943** | — Watson enters the University of Chicago. |
| **1947** | — Crick goes to Cambridge to work at Strangeways Laboratory. |
| **1949** | — Crick transfers to Cavendish Laboratory, Cambridge. |
| **1950** | — Watson graduates from Indiana University with a Ph.D. |
| **May 21–25, 1951** | — Watson meets Maurice Wilkins and sees the first image of X-ray crystallography. |
| **October 1951** | — Watson moves to Cambridge and meets Crick. |
| **November 26, 1951** | — Watson and Crick build a triple-helix model, which proves to be incorrect. |

| | |
|---|---|
| **1952** | — Peter Pauling receives a letter from his father, Linus Pauling, saying that the elder Pauling has found the structure of DNA. |
| **January 30, 1953** | — Watson visits King's College, London, and Wilkins shows him photo 51. Watson immediately recognizes that it is a helical structure, probably a double helix. |
| **February 28, 1953** | — While working with his cardboard cutouts of the four DNA bases, Watson hits upon the correct pairings. |
| **March 7, 1953** | — Watson and Crick finish assembling their large-scale model of DNA. |
| **April 25, 1953** | — Watson and Crick's paper, "Molecular Structure of Nucleic Acids," is published in the scientific journal *Nature*. |
| **May 30, 1953** | — Watson and Crick publish a second article in *Nature*, making further observations on how DNA works. |
| **1958** | — Rosalind Franklin dies of ovarian cancer, possibly caused by excessive exposure to X-rays. |
| **1962** | — Watson, Crick, and Wilkins share the Nobel Prize for Physiology or Medicine. |

| | |
|---|---|
| **1968** | — Watson's book *The Double Helix* is published. Watson becomes director of Cold Spring Harbor Laboratory. |
| **1988** | — Crick's book *What Mad Pursuit* is published. |
| **1989** | — Watson becomes the director of the Human Genome Project. |
| **1992** | — Watson resigns from the Human Genome Project. He becomes the president of Cold Spring Harbor Laboratory. |
| **July 28, 2004** | — Crick dies in San Diego, at age eighty-eight. |

# PRIMARY SOURCE TRANSCRIPTION

**Page 29: Notes written by Linus Pauling on November 26, 1952, as he tried to construct the nucleic acid structure.**

The $(PO_4)_3$ rings are nearly over one another

The P-O-H bond angles require that H be at z=o; i.e., on the level of P. Thus there are $(PO_4H)_3$ rings:

Diagram

I assume O layers 1.70 Å apart. both with and without P.

This makes O-O = 2.45 Å in $PO_4$
2.55 Å in 0-H...0
3.16 Å in plane
2.49 Å between $(PO_4)_3$ layers.

The last is too small. Probably $PO_4$'s are tipped.


**Page 35: The first page from Watson and Crick's second groundbreaking article, "Genetical Implications of the Structure of Deoxyribonucleic Acid," which appeared in *Nature* on May 30, 1953.**

Genetical Implications of the Structure of Deoxyribonucleic Acid
By J. D. Watson and F. H. C. Crick

Medical Research Council Unit for the Study of the Molecular Structure of Biological Systems, Cavendish Laboratory, Cambridge

The importance of deoxyribonucleic acid (DNA) within living cells is undisputed. It is found in all dividing cells, largely if not entirely in the nucleus, where it is an essential constituent of the chromosomes. Many lines of evidence indicate that it is the carrier of a part of (if not all) the genetic specificity of the chromosomes and thus of the gene itself.

Diagram

Fig. 1. Chemical formula of a single chain of deoxyribonucleic acid.

Fig. 2. This figure is purely diagrammatic. The two ribbons symbolize the two phosphate-sugar chains, and the horizontal rods the pairs of bases holding the chains together. The vertical line marks the fibre axis.

# GLOSSARY

**anatomist** Someone who studies the bodily structure of animals and plants.

**biology** The study of living organisms.

**chromosomes** Threadlike structures made of DNA and protein found in the nuclei of cells and containing genetic information.

**clone** An exact genetic replica of a DNA molecule, cell, tissue, organ, or entire plant or animal.

**DNA** Deoxyribonucleic acid; a long, thin molecule found in the nucleus of a cell.

**gene** A section of DNA containing a genetic code that causes a certain type of protein to be made.

**genetic** Having to do with genes or heredity.

**genetics** The study of heredity and the variation of inherited characteristics.

**genome** All of the genetic material in the nucleus of a cell.

**heredity** The passing on of physical or other traits through the genetic code from one generation to another.

**metabolism** All the chemical processes that can take place in a living organism that result in energy production.

**molecule** Two or more atoms bonded together to make a substance.

**organism** Any living thing.

**physics** The study of the properties and interactions of matter and energy.

**protein** Long-chained molecules used to build and repair cells.

**template** Something that is used as a pattern to create a copy.

# FOR MORE INFORMATION

The Biological Sciences Curriculum Study
5415 Mark Dabling Boulevard
Colorado Springs, CO  80918
(719) 531-5550
Web site: http://www.bscs.org/page.asp

Cold Spring Harbor Laboratory
P.O. Box 100
1 Bungtown Road
Cold Spring Harbor, NY 11724
(516) 367-8397
Web site: http://www.cshl.org

The Department of Molecular and Cellular Biology
Harvard University
7 Divinity Avenue
Cambridge, MA 02138
(617) 495-9924
Web site: http://www.mcb.harvard.edu/BioLinks.html

Human Genome Management Information System
Betty K. Mansfield
Oak Ridge National Laboratory (ORNL)
1060 Commerce Park, MS 6480
Oak Ridge, TN 37830
(865) 576-6669
Web site: http://www.ornl.gov/sci/techresources/Human_Genome/
home.shtml

The Salk Institute for Biological Studies
P.O. Box 85800
San Diego, CA 92186-5800
(858) 453-4100, ext. 1226
Web site: http://www.salk.edu

## Web Sites

Due to the changing nature of Internet links, the Rosen Publishing Group, Inc., has developed an online list of Web sites related to the subject of this book. This site is updated regularly. Please use this link to access the list:

http://www.rosenlinks.com/psrsdt/wcdna

# FOR FURTHER READING

## Books by Watson and Crick

Crick, Francis. *Life Itself*. New York: Simon & Schuster, 1981.

Watson, James D. *Genes, Girls, and Gamow: After the Double Helix*. New York: Knopf, 2002.

Watson, James D. *A Passion for DNA: Genes, Genomes, and Society*. Cold Spring Harbor, NY: Cold Spring Harbor Laboratory Press, 2001.

## Books by Other Authors

Perutz, Max. *I Wish I'd Made You Angry Earlier: Essays on Science, Scientists, and Humanity*. Cold Spring Harbor, NY: Cold Spring Harbor Laboratory Press, 2002.

Reilly, Philip R. *Abraham Lincoln's DNA and Other Adventures in Genetics*. Cold Spring Harbor, NY: Cold Spring Harbor Laboratory Press, 2000.

Ridley, Matt. *Nature Via Nurture: Genes, Experience, and What Makes Us Human*. New York: HarperCollins, 2003.

Witherly, Jeffre L., Galen P. Perry, and Darryl L. Leja. *An A to Z of DNA Science: What Scientists Mean When They Talk About Genes and Genomes*. Cold Spring Harbor, NY: Cold Spring Harbor Laboratory Press, 2001.

# BIBLIOGRAPHY

Clarke, Tom. "DNA's Family Tree." 2003. Retrieved April 21, 2004 (http://www.nature.com/nsu/030421/030421-5.html).

Crick, Francis. *What Mad Pursuit*. New York: Basic Books, 1988.

Genome News Network. "Genetic and Genomics Timeline." 2002–2004. Retrieved April 21, 2004 (http://www.genomenewsnetwork.org/timeline/timeline_home.shtml).

Lasker Medical Research Network. "James Watson Timeline." Retrieved April 21, 2004 (http://www.laskerfoundation.org/awards/kwood/watson/timeline.shtml).

National Centre for Biotechnology Education. "Double Helix: 1953–2003." 2004. Retrieved April 21, 2004 (http://www.ncbe.reading.ac.uk/DNA50/timeline.html).

Wade, Nicholas. "DNA, the Keeper of Life's Secrets, Starts to Talk." 2003. Retrieved April 21, 2004 (http://www.nytimes.com/2003/02/25/science/25HELI.html?ex=1082692800&en=b79c030ff28e3f25&ei=5070).

Watson, James D. *The Double Helix*. New York: Penguin Books, 1968.

Watson, James D. "Nobel Prize Banquet Speech." 1962. Retrieved April 21 2004 (http://www.nobel.se/medicine/laureates/1962/watson-speech.html).

# PRIMARY SOURCE IMAGE LIST

# INDEX

# Photo Credits

Front cover, p. 32 A. Barrington Brown/Photo Researchers, Inc.; back cover: Copernicus image © Library of Congress Prints and Photographs Division, Darwin image © Library of Congress Prints and Photographs Division, Hubble image courtesy Carnegie Observatories, The Carnegie Institution of Washington, Kepler image © Library of Congress Prints and Photographs Division, Mendel image © Pixtal/Superstock, Mendeleyev image © Edgar Fahs Smith Collection, University of Pennsylvania Library, Newton image © Library of Congress Prints and Photographs Division, Watson and Crick image © The James D. Watson Collection, Cold Spring Harbor Laboratory Archives; title page Kenneth Eward/BioGrafx/Photo Researchers, Inc.; pp. 5, 19, 25 *(left)*, 45 © Bettmann/Corbis; pp. 7, 12, 35 courtesy of the James D. Watson Collection, Cold Spring Harbor Laboratory Archives; p. 8 © Corbis; p. 10 Mary Evans Picture Library/Photo Researchers, Inc.; p. 15 © Getty Images; p. 17 © Yevgeny Khaldei/Corbis; pp. 23, 29, 31 From the Ava Helen and Linus Pauling Papers, Special Collections, Oregon State University; p. 25 *(right)* Photo Researchers, Inc.; p. 34 Wellcome Library, London; p. 38 Prof. G. Schatten/Photo Researchers, Inc.; p. 40 Biophoto Associates/Photo Researchers, Inc.; p. 41 National Human Genome Research Institute; p. 43 Carlyn Iverson/Photo Researchers, Inc.; p. 47 © Pierre Perrin/Corbis; p. 49 James King-Holmes/Photo Researchers, Inc.; p. 50 Hank Morgan/Photo Researchers, Inc.

# About the Author

Christy Marx has written for television, film, animation, computer games, and comic books. Christy lives in California with her lifemate and a horde of cats. Visit her Web site at www.christymarx.com.

Editor: Charles Hofer; Photo Researcher: Jeffrey Wendt